CLASSIC AFRICAN CHILDREN'S STORIES

CLASSIC AFRICAN CHILDREN'S STORIES

A COLLECTION OF

ANCIENT TALES

EDITED AND COMPILED BY

PHYLLIS SAVORY

A CITADEL PRESS BOOK
Published by Carol Publishing Group

I
DEDICATE
THIS BOOK TO ALL
WHO HAVE HELPED ME WITH THEIR
ENCOURAGEMENT TO WRITE THESE TALES · ALSO TO DUDUZILE
MKHIZE AND HER MOTHER MANALIMENI
MKHIZE WHO TOLD
THEM TO
ME

Carol Publishing Group Edition, 1995

Previously published as *Zulu Fireside Tales.*

A Citadel Press Book
Published by Carol Publishing Group
Citadel Press is a registered trademark of Carol Communications, Inc.
Editorial Offices: 600 Madison Avenue, New York, NY 10022
Sales & Distribution Offices: 120 Enterprise Avenue, Secaucus, NJ 07094
In Canada: Canadian Manda Group, One Atlantic Avenue, Suite 105
Toronto, Ontario, M6K 3E7

Queries regarding rights and permissions should be addressed to:
Carol Publishing Group, 600 Madison Avenue, New York, NY 10022

Manufactured in the United States of America
ISBN 0-8065-1704-2

10 9 8 7 6 5 4 3 2 1

Carol Publishing Group books are available at special discounts
for bulk purchases, sales promotions, fund raising, or
educational purposes. Special editions can also be created to
specifications. For details contact: Special Sales Department,
Carol Publishing Group, 120 Enterprise Ave., Secaucus, NJ 07094

The Cataloging-in-Publication Data for this title may be obtained
from the Library of Congress.

FOREWORD

I⊤ is with pleasure that I write a foreword to this little collection of Zulu tales, which tell of the adventures of Zulu children. Other children will love them, and their parents too will appreciate them for they have the authentic ring which one associates with a Zulu grand-mother graphically recounting them by the light of a flickering fire with a circle of children round her, listening intently and watching her every gesture.

Zulu stories speak of magic and cannibals and monsters and animals that talk. Quite a number of these, although their origin is Zulu, may be found with a variation in detail in the stories of other Bantu language groups.

In each language group will be found an animal that gets the better of the others when it comes to a contest of wits. Amongst the Sothos it is the Tortoise. The Xhosas give the palm to the Jackal, and the Shonas select the Hare, whilst the Zulus have a fabulous creature called Chakijana that plays tricks on everyone.

In this collection will be found all the ingredients that have been mentioned. For instance the magical and the mysterious, which bulk so largely in Zulu thought, are finely represented by the story of the five-headed snake which by the exercise of magic was turned into a handsome husband for Thandeka. It took more than a kiss to turn him into a prince. It could only be done by a deep knowledge of magic and its mysterious arts. The occult comes to the aid of Nomvula when she is captured by cannibals and a magic spear tells her how to escape, and when she falls into the hands of a second lot of cannibals she is saved by a frog that swallows her and carries her home.

The longing of baboons to possess a human child and their delight when they capture one and guard it, is a tradition that is very wide-spread amongst the Bantu and is told with variations in many tribes. This is also the case with the faithful herd boy whose favourite ox or cow is driven off by thieves who cannot, however, do anything with the animal without the boy's help. Eventually it submits to be killed and eaten, but the boy collects the bones and by means of magical words puts them all together again and restores the flesh, skin and life and rides off on it.

It is, however, not my function to retell the stories to the reader but such details as are here hinted at are quoted only to show how nearly the author has kept to a true representation of Zulu thought and custom, and to their traditional manner of telling the tales.

Since the time of Dr. Henry Callaway, whose collection appeared in 1872, many others have written similar tales, but there are still more to be told and it is to be hoped that Phyllis Savory will give us another sample, for she possesses the art of telling them.

D. McK. Malcolm.

University of Natal,
  Durban.

CONTENTS

INTRODUCTION

IF you will take out a map of South Africa and mark the land that falls within a radius of latitude 32.5 East and longitude 38 degrees South, you will find a large area known as ZULULAND. In this country, from 1818 to 1828, the great chief, Chaka, ruled his people with a rod of iron. It was a nation of strong men and brave warriors, some of whose customs were both strange and barbaric.

When the white people came to settle in this part of Africa, there was a great deal of bloodshed on both sides. The Zulu Impis (armies) ranged both far and wide, and Natal and other lands around were overrun by their fierce warriors until they decided to lay down their shields and spears and become the peaceful nation they are today.

Before and during all this fighting, and afterwards too, it was their custom, as they sat at night around the fires in their huts, to tell their folk tales. In this way the stories passed from one generation to another.

Now that their children are taught to read and write, the old custom of the "Fireside Tales" is dying out and, with education, the tales themselves are being lost to memory. Indeed, it is from only a few natives that one can hear these stories today.

Hence I was fortunate a year ago to have a little Zulu girl come to work for me. Her name was Duduzele, and as I gained her confidence, the tales spilled out. When I had run *her* stock dry, I asked her to find me more, and she brought her mother to me. The old woman was most co-operative and delved far into her childhood days. She came to see me many times and, one by one, through the smoke of years, the tales came back to her.

I have endeavored to tell these stories from the point of view of the Zulu people. To appreciate them fully, the reader must realize that when these tales originated, the people from whose lips they came had blood, death and cruelty as their daily lot, and they also believed strongly in witchcraft. Cannibalism, for instance, is a word that is only a memory of the past to them now, but long ago there *were* natives who ate human flesh. These much dreaded people went by the name of the Amazimuzimu. In these stories they take the place of the wicked ogres in our European tales.

P. S. W.

8

1

NTUNJAMBILI

In far away days in Zululand there lived a worthy couple, Zondi and his wife Nobamba. They tilled their fields and sowed their crops, and their grain pits overflowed. The good God blessed their cattle so that they multiplied and brought them wealth, but in spite of this their hearts were sad, for no child was born to them to share their good fortune and their love.

Regularly they consulted their nearby witch doctors, and regularly they drank the magic potions with which they were provided, but still no child was born; and thus time wore on and on.

At last, after many years, they knew that their wish was to be fulfilled and great was their rejoicing and their thankfulness. But when the birth took place, their joy was killed, for twins were born, and this, in bygone days, was a calamity and a disgrace in their land, and looked upon as a forerunner of misfortune.

Carefully they hid the truth from all around, for the Zulu law demanded that twins should be killed at birth.

Time and again they tried to steel themselves to carry out the law, but each time, as the tiny hands clasped their mother's breast, their courage died within them. So they hid one of the babies, and when friends came to visit, showed them only one.

They called the boy Demana and his little sister Demazana.

9

Their deceit worked well to begin with, but as time passed, they found it more and more difficult to keep their secret from their friends and their chief.

They therefore decided to move their home to a wild and lonely place where a swiftly flowing river passed through a rocky gorge, and later past a huge dome-shaped rock called "Ntunjambili" that towered to the skies.

This rock was split from top to bottom, as though some great bolt of lightning had struck it. Some said that strange songs and mutterings had been heard within it, and more than once, others said, the crack had been seen to widen, and then close again. Ntunjambili was therefore looked upon with awe, and none went that way by choice. Because of this Zondi and Nobamba felt that their babies would be safer in their new home, and all went well for a while.

The twins were six years old when great trouble struck the land. Nearly all the cattle died from some mysterious disease; the fertile land was scorched and dried by a cruel drought, and lastly, disease broke out among the people themselves.

In time the chief called a meeting of the tribe, and told them that his witch doctors would meet at noon the following day to "smell" the culprit out, for someone must have done a great wrong to bring such sorrow to them all.

Zondi and Nobamba felt sure that their disobedience to the law in hiding the birth of twins would now be found out, and a great fear seized them.

Sorrowfully Zondi took little Demana and Demazana down to the swiftly flowing river, and there, one after the other, he threw them in.

With his hand pressed over his eyes, so that he would not see them sink, he wept as he stumbled blindly up the bank, and fled to the comfort of his wife.

But the good God was watching over the little ones; Demana grasped his sister's hand as she was washed against him, and a kindly current bore them downriver to an overhanging branch, which Demana caught in passing.

He was a strong little boy, and, with great presence of mind in one so young, he held grimly on to both Demazana and to the

SYLVIA BAXTER.

11

branch. Another swirl of water washed them against a shallow bank, and there he clambered out onto the dry land, dragging his little sister with him.

They sat for a while in the sunshine to warm their chilled bodies and to recover from their fright.

Now Fate had landed them directly beneath Ntunjambili, and, as they sat wondering what to do, they heard a creak behind them, and turned to see the great rock open from top to bottom, while from the cavern deep within, there came soft singing, and a troupe of "Nunus" came out in single file.

"Demana and Demazana, welcome to our home," they cried. "Come in and live with us. All sad hearts are mended here." Whereupon they shepherded the children into a large and softly lighted cavern.

They gazed about them in wonder, and saw that all around were little creatures of the underworld, and the softly glowing light came from millions of little glow-worms and fireflies that clung to the high domed ceiling.

This was indeed a place of love and kindness. All the broken and sad of heart took refuge here and the little Nunus nursed their hurts. They found small beetles with broken legs being tended with loving care; lizards with broken tails; an orphaned baby fawn whose mother had fallen victim to the dreaded lion's claws; an eagle with a broken wing. All were welcome there, and the comradeship among them grew.

Gladly the children stayed in this haven of peace and refuge, and came to look upon it as their home.

They lived on mushrooms that grew around the walls and on honey that trickled through from some great bees' nest in a crevice in the rock above them. Wild fruits, too, their little hosts gathered from the forest, and brought to them.

The Nunus taught them to say "Open, open, oh, rock Ntunjambili," (*Vula, vula, litche lika Ntunjambili*) when they wished to walk abroad. On this command Ntunjambili opened to let them out. Daily they walked along the riverbank, hand in hand, and life was full of happiness. They grew to love their little Nunu friends, and no longer wished to return to their home, for in their minds was always the thought of how their father had tried to kill them.

During all this time Zondi and Nobamba daily mourned the loss of their little ones, and Zondi would often walk along the riverbank in case some miracle had saved them.

On one such walk he saw the great rock open up and the twins come out, laughing and singing as they ran to paddle in the shallows of the pool that had given them back to life.

At first he thought he would call to them, but on second thoughts he hid and watched as they splashed and played in the water.

Soon they tired of their fun, and as they left the water, he saw the great rock open up once more, and the little Nunus come to call them in.

He hurried home to tell Nobamba, who was beside herself with joy, and begged him to go and fetch the children home.

Day after day he walked up and down the riverbank beside the great rock, but it was many months before he again saw the twins playing in the pool. This time he went to them, and begged them to come home to their mother. So, with a small hand clasped in each of his, he led them to Nobamba.

But although she bestowed on them all the mother love she had given to them in the past, they had lost their love of home, and they yearned for the little Nunus, who had saved them in their time of trouble; and for all their strange underground friends.

13

Thus it was that one night when darkness came and their father. and mother slept, Demana took his sister by the hand, and the two slipped silently from the hut; and as the bright moon shone on the old familiar scene, they threaded their way through the bush to the river. There, hand in hand, they stood before Ntunjambili, and in the soft, sweet voice of childhood sang to the rock,

"Litshe lika Ntunjambili!	*"Rock, rock, rock, Ntunjambili,*
Litshe lika Ntunjambili!	*Open, I want to get in.*
Ngivulele ngingene.	*If you won't open to me*
Alivulwa ngabantu,	*Then open to the swallows*
Livulwa yizinkonjane,	*That we see flying above.*
Zona zindiza phezulu."	*Open, I want to get in."*

The crack in the huge rock gradually widened in obedience to their words and the soft murmur of voices came to them as the little Nunus greeted them at the opening with,

"Come in, Demana and Demazana, we have been lonely without you." This murmur burst into a chorus of song as all the little creatures of the underworld welcomed them home.

Thus they live to this day, helping the Nunus to tend the hurts and sorrows of the little people in the heart of Ntunjambili.

2

THE ADVENTURES OF NOMVULA

NOMVULA was a little Xhosa girl. She lived with her mother and father at the foot of a towering hill up which she and her little friends often went to play.

There was a tiny crystal-clear lake at the end of the long climb, and in it they would cool their shiny brown bodies in the heat of the midday sun.

On one such day the children splashed and played beyond the normal time and, as the shadows lengthened, they realized with a start that it was almost time for the evening meal. So down the twisting, rocky path they scampered as the sun dipped behind the hill.

When nearly home, Nomvula discovered that she had left the pretty new bead loin strap that her mother had made for her with such care on a big flat rock where they had rested between their games.

Now, apart from a braided goatskin which she slung across her shoulders from time to time, this was her first bit of clothing and finery; for in the golden weather of her country there was no need of clothes for one so young.

"Cousin," she cried to the girl in front of her, "please come back with me to fetch my buhlalu, which I have left behind! My mother will beat me if I return without it." But no one would help her, so she turned back alone along the winding path, and the last that her companions saw of her was a little brown figure climbing into the mist that was settling like a great white cloth over the hill.

Nomvula came at last to the big flat rock, and there to her great joy was her pretty buhlalu. She tied it round her waist, and turned to take the homeward path, but the mist was all around her, and in her haste she missed the path, and took the one beyond it.

Down the hill she skipped and ran, but soon she stopped, uncertain which way to go, and found that she was completely lost.

As the darkness deepened she wandered on, and in time she saw a little hut with a light shining through an open doorway. Joyfully she hurried on, and soon stood in the doorway to ask for a night's refuge.

Great was her surprise to find a large and shaggy hyena sitting on a stool in front of a warm and cozy fire.

"Who are you, to visit me at such an hour?" asked the hyena, as she was about to run away. "Come in and share my meal." He spoke kindly, and little Nomvula was so cold and near to tears that she thankfully crept into the warmth of the hut. The hyena got up and quickly closed and fastened the door behind her.

"One stipulation I must make," he continued, "and that is that you remain here as my servant, and cook my food for me."

"But I have not learned to cook," Nomvula answered tearfully.

"COOK MY FOOD," the hyena snarled in quite a different voice, "or you will feel the sharpness of my teeth!" So with trembling hands Nomvula built up the fire, and set the pot to boil. Thus, under the hyena's directions, the meal was cooked, and they

15

sat and ate together, then settled down to sleep.

Now, when the sun came up, the hyena took his herd of cattle out to graze, telling Nomvula to wash the wooden milking pails and have everything ready when he brought them back at milking time. However, as soon as he had gone, she crept through the long grass, and, when out of sight, ran as fast as her little legs would carry her in the direction of her home.

Just as she thought she recognized the hill in front of her, she she met a party of Mazimuzimu women (cannibals) with pots of water on their heads.

"Ah," said the leader, putting down her pot, "here is food for us today," and they at once commenced to chase Nomvula.

As they were gaining on her, she saw another group of women, hoeing in a field, so ran to them for help.

"Leave the child alone," they cried, brandishing their hoes at her pursuers, "this land belongs to us, and you trespass here."

They took Nomvula by the hand, and led her to a hut. There they pushed her roughly in, shutting the door behind her, and she realized that she had fallen from one lot of cannibals to another.

While she sat wondering what to do, one of the long, thin native spears that was leaning against the wall bent down to her and said, "If you will do as I say, I will save you. Come close to me, and let me shave your head."

Then with careful sweeps of his razor-sharp blade the magic spear shaved off all Nomvula's hair. This it divided into three parts, telling her to throw one part into the nearby pool from which the women drew the drinking water; the second part on the ground where the fire would be made to roast her; and the third part on the rubbish heap.

When this was done, she made all haste to escape once more through the long grass in the direction of her home.

Soon the women returned from gathering the wood to cook their feast, and as they approached the hut, they called, "Nomvula, come here." Now the magic spear had bewitched Nomvula's hair, and it answered from the pool, "I am here." The women hurried to the pool. They could find no sign of Nomvula there, so all ran back to the hut calling out again, "Nomvula, come here!"

"I am here," answered the second lot of hair from the clearing

near the woodpile, and all the women rushed to *this* voice. Again
they could see no trace of Nomvula, so for the third time they
called, "Nomvula, come here!"

This time the magic voice came from the rubbish heap and they
rushed in that direction. Thus it was some time before they realized
that they had been tricked; and Nomvula was a long way down
the path that led across the river toward her home before they set
off in pursuit.

Unfortunately, however, her little legs soon began to tire,
and when she heard the yells of joy as her pursuers gained on her,
she made for the friendly waters of the river, preferring to be
drowned rather than fall into the hands of the cruel Mazimuzimu
women.

SYLVIA BAXTER -

At last she reached the bank and threw herself into the water.
Here, a kindly frog heard her cries for help, so he opened his great
mouth and swallowed her, taking care to keep his lips slightly open
so that she could breathe.

"Eh! but where is she?" cried the leading Mazimuzimu. "It
was *here* that she jumped in," pointing to a little ridge under which
the frog had his home. Thereupon they all waded into the water,

poking about with the long sticks that they carried. All they found was a fat old frog that grumbled and muttered at them from his hole under the bank, and in time the Mazimuzimu went home, very much annoyed at their loss.

As soon as they were out of sight, the frog crept out of the river, and commenced his long trip to Nomvula's home. The heavy load he carried slowed him down, for with Nomvula in his stomach he could no longer hop.

After some time he met two men coming toward him, and he heard one say, "Look at Selesele, he surely is the grandfather of all frogs. Let us kill him with our spears."

At this, the frog called out, "Do not kill me. I carry Nomvula to her home."

"Nomvula?" said the taller of the two. "I had a daughter of that name, but she is gone. I would not hurt one who spoke her name," and they passed on.

Farther along the road he met two women returning from hoeing the fields, and one said to the other,

"Eh, but a Bad One walks toward us. Let us kill him with our hoes."

The frog replied, "Do not hurt me. I carry Nomvula to her home."

"Nomvula?" asked one of the women. "I had a daughter of that name, my only child, and her name is sweet to me. We will let you live," and they passed him by.

In time he reached Nomvula's home, where her grandmother was sweeping the yard. As she saw the great frog crawling along toward her she raised her broom to sweep him from her sight. But Selesele said,

"Please do not hurt me. I carry Nomvula to her home."

"Nomvula?" cried the grandmother, "she was my pretty one, my littlest one. All who speak her name are welcome here. See, I will build you a house, and I will care for you forever."

She thereupon swept a little clearing beneath a bush, and commenced to lace the branches with saplings for a roof, as a home for Selesele.

While she was doing this, Nomvula's father came home from his hunt, and the frog turned to him and said,

18

"I have brought Nomvula to her home. How will you reward me if I give her back to you?"

"If you have brought back our little one to us," he said, "all my money is yours."

But Selesele replied, "Money? No, 'tis hard on the teeth and heavy in the belly. I have no use for such."

"Perchance a goat would be a fitting gift?" the father asked.

"A *goat*, in exchange for your daughter? No, my reward will be the fattest cow in your herd. It is long since I ate my fill of tender beef. But I wish it slaughtered, cleaned and the meat laid out upon the skin. Then will I call my friends and we will drag it home."

The agreement was made, whereupon Selesele with a great arching of his body opened his mouth, and brought forth Nomvula, who was none the worse for her adventures. Furthermore, when the bargain on the father's side was fulfilled, Selesele called his friends, and, as night came down, they dragged their feast off into the darkness.

3

THE WICKED MAZIMUZIMU

WHILE their father worked in the faraway mines of Johannesburg, little Ncinci and her brother Mvemve lived with their mother in the hills of Zululand.

Maluzwane was a good mother. Her hut was clean and neat. Her little ones were plump, and glossy from the lion fat that was weekly rubbed into their strong young bodies. Lion fat, of course, was scarce, but all knew that the fat of the "Great One of the Forest" was indeed good medicine for strength and beauty. She spared nothing in their care.

Clothes were the least of her worries. Ncinci wore a little beaded segege (short string skirt, with a bead at the end of each string). Mvemve was even easier to clothe, for he wore nothing at all.

Daily they played with their little black neighbours, modeling small clay oxen, bathing in the nearby river, trapping birds—in fact, all the games that small black children play.

One day the girls and boys parted company in their fun. Ncinci and the other girls decided on some river games and went down to bathe.

The boys took a bag of grain to use as bait, and went to trap birds in the nearby hills to roast for their midday meal.

Soon there came shouts of fun and laughter from the river as the girls tumbled about in the water and ducked each other; while from the hills there slowly arose a long, thin spiral of smoke as the boys prepared a fire on which to roast the birds they had caught.

While the fun was at its highest, little Ncinci's segege string came undone, and her lovely new skirt went floating down the river, bobbing and swirling as the swiftly running water carried it away.

"Oh!" she cried, "my lovely new segege!" and she turned to the girl nearest to her and said, "Please help me to catch it, before it is lost to me."

But her little friend replied,

"It is no affair of mine."

So Ncinci turned to one of the bigger girls and said, "*Please* help me to catch my segege, your legs are longer than mine."

Once more she was told to catch her own property, and as it bobbed farther and farther from view, Ncinci commenced to weep, and ran splashing through the shallow water after it. But always it eluded her.

Once her hand was on it! But, no, a wicked swirl of water plucked it from her fingers as they were about to close on it.

"Ei," she said, "the water holds me back. My legs move faster on the land." So she scrambled up the bank and ran across to a shallow ford she knew around the river bend to await her segege there.

By this time she was far from the sight of her friends and too intent on the rescue of her pretty little skirt to notice a tall black man with a bag slung over his shoulder approach from down the river-bank.

"Why are you running so fast, my little one?" asked the stranger.

"*Please* help me get my segege!" she begged, pointing to the little black object still bobbing up and down as the current carried it onward.

"That is quickly done," he replied, striding into the water. Joy! he had it in his hand, and little Ncinci danced with pleasure

SYLVIA BAXTER.

as he carried it safely to her side.

But as she stretched up her hand to take it from him, the stranger caught her roughly and pushed her into his bag. Too terrified to scream, she realized that she was in the hands of one of the dreaded Mazimuzimus (cannibals) who searched the hills for lone and straying children.

"Please, *please*, let me out," she pleaded.

"Oh, no," he replied. "It is long since I found one as plump as you. At home a fire crackles for my evening meal," and he slung her over his shoulder, leaving the river behind him as he climbed the hills to his home.

But Ncinci was heavy and he was hungry, so when he saw a long, thin spiral of smoke climbing to the skies, he thought he would go that way and maybe beg a bite of food.

In time he reached a slanting rock beneath whose shelter Mvemve and his friends were roasting the birds that they had caught. Seeing only children there, he boldly approached and said,

"Good morning, little brothers. I have come from far afield, and it is long since I have eaten. Let me eat with you, and I will make my magic bag sing to you."

Now, magic of all kinds is what every black child loves, so they shared their meal with the tall stranger, and when they had eaten, asked for their reward.

He then went up to the bag, saying, "Sing, bag, sing," and prodded it with his finger.

Whereupon Ncinci called out,

"I am Ncinci, I am Ncinci, and my brother is Mvemve, my brother is Mvemve."

"Truly yours is a wonderful magic," said the clever Mvemve, hiding his shock at hearing his sister's voice. "Such magic is worth more than these few roast birds. If you will come with me to my mother's home, she will give you a juicy steak from the ox she killed but yesterday. I will go ahead and beg her to prepare a meal for you." And he raced down the hillside to warn his mother of his coming. Thus it was that when the Mazimuzimu reached her hut, she had made her plans.

She greeted him with a great show of pleasure, bade him put his load in the shade of a nearby tree, and asked him to fetch some water in which to cook his meal.

No sooner had he set off for the river than Maluzwane quickly opened the bag, and hid Ncinci in the goat pen. She then made all haste to a swarm of bees that hung from a nearby tree; popped the bag over them, shook them carefully in, and tied it up once more.

Quickly she hung it from the rafters of her hut, and as soon as the smoke from the fire had made the bees stupid and drowsy, she replaced it beneath the tree.

Now when the Mazimuzimu dipped the can with which Maluzwane had provided him into the river, he found that the water ran out of many holes in its sieve-like bottom. He therefore found some clay, and one by one he plastered up the holes.

This took some time to do, and when at last he reached the cooking hut, all was ready for his feast. Having eaten his fill, he once more slung the load over his shoulders, and bidding his hostess goodbye, continued on his way.

"Wife," he cried as he neared his home, "bring out the biggest cooking pot, and bring me lots of firewood while I prepare the feast. Come in and close the door so that none can see," he continued, as his wife and child followed him into the hut.

He put down his load at the entrance, and while he sharpened an evil-looking knife, he bade his child carry the feast into the hut. However, no sooner had the child laid hands on it, than the bees stung him through the cloth. With a cry of pain he dropped it in the middle of the hut, and refused to touch it again.

"Very well," the Mazimuzimu cried. "I will feast alone. Get out!" Whereupon he chased both wife and child away. "Those who cannot help cannot eat!" he added, with a chuckle.

Then he blocked the windows and barred the door, and, with wicked, gloating eyes, he himself undid the string.

The bees were now awake and very angry. They flew straight for his head, and there they settled, and there they stung him as he tried wildly to unfasten the battened door.

In time he gained the open, and with screams of pain he raced headlong to a muddy pool. Into the sticky mud he plunged his burning head. And there he stuck, feet in the air. And there the mud choked and suffocated the wicked Mazimuzimu while the mother and son laughed with glee!

4

THE SON OF THE TORTOISE

THE rains were very late, and the whole countryside was parched and dry. The cattle were hollow-eyed and thin, as they eagerly licked the mud, the only moisture that was left, in the nearby river bed.

"The Spirit of the River is angry," the old men muttered among themselves. "Maybe a gift would bring forth water for our beasts and ourselves to drink."

Dinga, the little herd boy, listened to their talk, and at noon the following day as his cattle licked the mud, he said,

"Oh, River, the best black ox in my father's herd I bring to you today. He is yours if you will let the water up for all to drink." But no water came, and the thirsty beasts mooed in their despair.

"Maybe," Dinga continued, "a red bull would please you more? Here is one, the best in all the land. Take him, and fill the pool for all to drink." Still the water refused to come.

Now there was one among the herd, a milk-white flawless cow, the pride of his father's heart. This cow he drove forward from the rest.

"Take 'Mhlophe,' and my father's heart goes with her—only let the water come!" pleaded Dinga. But the cracks in the hard, dry river bed seemed to widen as they smiled their refusal at his bribe.

In despair he searched his mind for something that would please. Then he said to the river,

"I have a little sister at my father's house. A laughing, fat, and happy child. Even *her* will I give to you if you will quench the thirst of all!"

As the words left his lips, the water bubbled up, crystal-clear, and filled the pool for all to drink.

After a time Dinga went home to fetch his little sister, telling her that they would play beneath the trees that fringed the river-bank. This they did until Nompofo fell asleep, her cheek upon her little hands. Then Dinga stole away, leaving her in fulfilment of his work.

Soon she awoke, and as she did so, the Spirit of the River rose up out of the water to claim his reward. But Nompofo was so terrified at the sight of one so strange that, with a scream that echoed through the hills, she ran as fast as her fat little legs would carry her, and in time she escaped him.

She wandered on and on among the hills, but could not find her home. Finally, as night approached, a well-kept field of mabele (Kaffir corn) came in sight.

"Ah," she thought, "someone *must* live here!" But she was wrong, for she had wandered far from her own chief's land into the adjoining animal kingdom, and the field belonged to Ndlovu (the elephant), their king.

By this time she was very hungry, so she made herself a little shelter in a thicket near the lands, and went to gather some ripe mabele. This she crushed between two flat stones, made a fire, and prepared herself a meal. Then, covering herself with branches and grass, she went to sleep.

SYLVIA BAXTER.

Early next morning she heard talking and laughter nearby and peeping from her little "hide," she saw the elephant's animal servants collecting the ripe mabele for their king.

Soon she heard one say! "Alert, alert! There is danger close at hand. Can you not smell a foreign smell?" And they all put their noses in the air and sniffed.

Then another one exclaimed, "A thief has stolen our lord Ndlovu's grain. See where the ripened fruit has been torn down!" And they all stamped their feet, and turned this way and that, but nowhere could they see the thief.

Now, as they neared the thicket where Nompofo hid, she blew her smouldering fire to a blaze, and set the mabele field alight, to drive the beasts away.

In panic they all raced before the flames to report to Ndlovu, calling out, "My lord, my lord, a thief is in your fields!"

"My lord, my lord, your lands are all ablaze!"

The elephant was angry at being disturbed at such an early hour, especially when he saw that his servants had come empty-handed from the lands. So he called the jackal to him and said,

"Go you who sing to the moon, and kill this creature that has dared to spoil my lands," So Mpungushe (the jackal), bushy tail dragging on the ground, nervously looking over his shoulder from time to time, unwillingly returned to the field.

There he poked his sharp nose first into one bush and then into another until he finally came to the thicket where Nompofo hid.

"I am Mpungushe," he called out nervously, "the bold and cunning Mpungushe. Come out and let me kill you!"

But Nompofo, making her voice as deep and as fierce as she could, replied, "How should I fear one as small as you? I am Nompofo! It is well known that my horns are branched like a tree, with ten sharp points to run you through, ten of such as you would fit comfortably in my mouth. Be ready, for I am coming out!"

The jackal gave a piercing yell and, with his bushy tail well between his legs, bolted back to Ndlovu's hut without once looking back.

"My lord, my lord," he cried, "a wicked giant is in your land, I saw him. He is taller than the trees. Even you he could crush beneath his foot."

27

There was silence among the animals while the elephant flapped his great ears backward and forward in distress.

At last one spoke, "It would take more than a giant to crush me," boasted Fudu, the tortoise. "*I* will rid you of your enemy!" And he swaggered down the path toward the field while they all craned their necks to watch.

Now, Nompofo was really very frightened and near to tears. When she heard Fudu thudding along the path toward her, making all the clatter he could with his heavy shell, singing loudly as

he came, "I am the son of my father, I am the son of my father," she could hide her fear no longer, and, bursting from her hiding place, ran screaming into the forest. At this Fudu sat for a long time in the pathway and laughed and laughed and laughed!

At last, he thought, Mpungushe had shown himself in his true colors—the coward of the veld, frightened of a little child who had lost her way! He determined, however, to keep this to himself, so as not to belittle his own daring.

He waddled back to Ndlovu with his thumbs stuck under his armpits, still singing loudly, "I am the son of my father; the mighty giant has fled at the sight of the brave and bold Fudu! I am the son of my father."

There was great rejoicing in the kingdom of Ndlovu at Fudu's victory over such a dangerous enemy, and in his gratitude the elephant made the tortoise his chief counselor while Mpungushe was banished from the land for his cowardice.

Since his downfall the jackal has never had the courage to hunt for himself, but follows the lion, eating the scraps that he leaves— and crying to the moon!

5

MAKHANDA MAHLANU OR THE FIVE HEADS

A LONG time ago there was a powerful king who ruled all the snakes. His body was like that of any other snake, but of a tremendous size, and his strength was as the strength of ten.

All birds, beasts, and humans feared him, for, besides his size and strength, he had five heads, each one separate. Each could speak for itself, and each had a cunning of its own.

Now for many years the snake people had hoped for an heir to the throne to bring blessings to their kingdom, and to guide them when their present ruler died.

Makhanda Mahlanu (Five Heads), however, had no wish to marry, though throughout his reign the snake mothers had anxiously brought their slim-hipped daughters for his choice. None of the graceful damsels pleased him. He wished for one whose head was carried high, so that as his queen she would be better able to see what happened in the far corners of his kingdom. Thus she could help him rule.

The cobra family felt that in the end the honor would be theirs. Hence they taught their young ones to stand higher and yet higher. As you know, a cobra can almost reach a man's height, when with great hood spread it stands erect to strike its victim down.

But one by one the king turned the cobra maids away, and in time the Elders of the snake court called a meeting to discuss the matter, and to persuade him to take a wife.

"Our lord," they cried, "who will rule us when you die? Surely from among our many clans, one damsel can be found to fill your heart with love?"

"Love," cried the king. "Who can love a heart that has no warmth in it? What cold-blooded maid could love five heads at once? Surely this is beyond a reptile's stony heart?

"No, I have looked in vain," he continued. "No one in my kingdom can fulfil my needs. I will wed a human maid. Think what honour this will bring both to me and to my kingdom! A human wife has never yet belonged to one of us. Send out my messengers to all the human chiefs around, and let them know

29

that there will be death to any maiden who refuses the honor I would bestow on her. See that my wish is made known far and wide."

So the word went out to all around, and great was the fear and sorrow among the human maids. Day by day the long, thin messengers went searching. Each maiden, as she refused the dreadful offer of a serpent crown, was strangled without pity, and the life choked out of her.

Soon, so great was the distress among the people far and near that a meeting was called, and all drew lots to find the snake a fitting human bride to end the dreadful fear.

At last the bones were thrown, and it fell to the lot of Thandeka (the loved one) to pay the price, to bring peace and security once more to her friends.

With a great beating of drums, the messengers took back her promise to wed their king. But there was no beating of drums in Thandeka's home, where all were full of sorrow and despair. However, without complaint they held their heads high as they helped her to make her bridal beadwork, and to mould the cooking pots befitting a bride.

When all was ready, they sent a messenger to Makhanda Mahlanu saying that her father and her two uncles would escort her to his home.

"No," said the snake, "I will come to fetch my bride from her father's hut in the proper manner. But," he added, "I will not enter by a human door. That way lies danger. Make holes for me in the roof of the hut. By one of these will I enter to claim my bride and let no one be in sight."

In this manner, preparations were made to receive the king of snakes.

All was done as he had commanded, and at noon, on the appointed day Makhanda Mahlanu came gliding down the pathway that led to the bridal kraal.

On each of his five heads was placed a royal crown, and as he slid along the five heads darted hither and thither, and the five split tongues eagerly licked their stone-cold lips, as he thought of the lovely human bride.

Makhanda Mahlanu found a knotted tree trunk that leaned

against the marriage hut, and this he climbed with haste. With quick eyes darting here and there, he found a hole prepared for him in the thatch.

"This is well," he said. "No doors for *me*," and he slithered through the gap. The drop to the floor was higher than he had expected, but, once inside the hut, he licked his many lips once more and looked around for his bride.

To his great anger, the hut was empty. Had he been tricked? He tried to leap back to the hole in the roof, to make his escape before it was too late. It was just too high. The door? The place where the door had been was blocked, and there was no escape that way.

A great hiss of rage came from his five divided tongues as he saw smoke creeping through the thatch, heard the crackling of flames, and realized that he was trapped..

He thrashed about in helpless rage, but soon the great licking flames covered the whole hut, and he sank senseless to the ground.

"Ah, Thandeka, now my task begins," said the girl's father, as he searched among the ashes of the hut. "Quickly, bring my magic pot," and with care he gathered the ashes of the royal snake, and put them in the pot.

Next, he took some spittle from his mouth, and this he mixed with the ashes of the snake, singing, as he did so, a strange and solemn song.

When the song was ended, he carried the pot to a pond nearby and placed it in the water, the top just showing, and quickly returned to the ruins of the hut.

There he built a fire, and on it scattered parings from his fingernails; and all night long he sat as in a trance. As daylight came he turned to the pond.

"Ah, it works," he cried, as he saw, slowly rising from the pot, two human hands, followed by a pair of strong and shapely arms. He returned to the hut and took no food or drink for all that day, and sat as though in death.

Then, as darkness came again, he arose and built a second fire. Then, as the flames leaped up, he sprinkled on them blood from his own blood stream, and all night long he sat and watched.

Once more as dawn appeared he turned to the pond. This time

he saw arising from between the arms a single human head, and he saw the scales fall from the glassy reptile eyes. Soon there came a nose, and after that a mouth of strength and kindness.

"It works, it works!" he cried again with joy. "My task is nearly done." Whereupon he returned to the ruins of the hut once more and neither ate nor drank throughout the day, sitting as if turned to stone.

Now, as the darkness came, for the third and last time he built his fire, and this time he breathed on the flames breath from his own lungs, and again he sat the whole night through.

For the third time, as the dawn came, he looked towards the pond and a cry of still greater joy came from his lips, For there, stepping out of the magic pot, was a man of strength and beauty, a fitting bridegroom for Thandeka's hand.

"Welcome, my son," the old man said, "we are of one flesh, you and I. Your human heart now beats with love." And, taking him by the hand, he led him to Thandeka's hut.

Then he called all the tribes from far and near and great was

the wedding feast that followed. There was much rejoicing at the happy ending to their time of fear.

Since that time the Snake People have gone leaderless. They no longer live an ordered life, but dwell in holes and trees although the cobras still think that *theirs* should be the royal line, and they proudly raise their heads on high.

SYLVIA BAXTER.

6

NKALIMEVA

In the big wild spaces of Africa there are many kingdoms, and many sovereigns rule the creatures of the wilds.

In one such kingdom, Ndlovu (the elephant) ruled as king and lord of all. He was wise and good and kind, and all his subjects looked up to him with love and admiration. They boasted of his greatness far and wide. The Nkau (monkeys), always chatterboxes who could not mind their own business, were continually chiding the animals of the adjoining kingdoms for their lack of law and order.

"You should have one of the clan of Ndlovu to rule you," they taunted, aiming overripe fruit at all who crossed their border. "When hunger threatens, our king warns us to fill our larders. When drought strikes, he bores holes in the river bed with his long and clever trunk, and the water oozes up for all to drink. Great, great *GREAT* is the wisdom of Ndlovu."

They swung from the branches of the highest trees, chattering, laughing, and so carefree that the animals from the adjoining kingdom said,

"That is a land of song and laughter. Surely the Nkau speak the truth. *Our* lord was never thus, for when the great drought struck, *he* was the first to starve and die. We have been leaderless too long. Let us send Nkalimeva to tempt Ndlovu to be our king. Who but we have the great broad moba (sugar cane) fields? It is well known that he loves sweet things above all else.

"We will send a messenger to him with a dozen of our sweetest sticks to tempt him from his land."

They searched the cane fields for their bribe, and tied them round with creepers from the trees, and with this bundle they loaded Nkalimeva and sent him on his way.

It was the daily duty of Ndlovu's subjects to gather food for their lord, and bring it to his hut; green saplings from the trees, bundles of juicy grass, and, in season, fruit from the trees. All vied to bring their king the choicest fare.

Now, as Nkalimeva travelled deeper into the rival kingdom with his load, he scattered chips of sugar cane along the way. Those who crossed his pathway smelled its luscious sweetness and gathered up the pieces for their lord. Never had its equal come his way or theirs.

The king was pleased, "I'll have more of this sweetness," he said. "Go find me more!"

This time, however, all his subjects searched in vain while Nkalimeva hid from view. When he felt the time was ripe, he approached the kraal where the animals lived.

"My lord Ndlovu," he purred, as his forehead touched the ground in humble greeting, "I bring you gifts from far away. Our lands are ripe, our pits are full, and this sweetness lies rotting on the ground."

As everyone knows, an elephant's greed is great. Ndlovu welcomed the stranger to his hut, and day by day Nkalimeva fed him sugar cane until the last sweet stick had gone. On that day, when his subjects brought *their* daily offerings, the elephant said roughly, "Your boughs and grass are stale and withered. Find me more of this luscious cane!"

35

SYLVIA BAXTER.

This was just what Nkalimeva wanted, and he broke in,
"Allow *me* to find your food for you today, my lord, I can find you moba cane. Let your people rest."

With a sigh of relief the elephant's subjects went to their resting ground in the shade of the trees to sleep, for their searchings had tired them.

When they had gone, Nkalimeva said to the king, "My lord, over the hill beyond the river that bounds your kingdom are fields and fields of the sweet moba cane. I could carry but a little at a time for you. Come with me, and there you can daily eat your fill." And so they set off together.

Now, when the evening came, and his subjects had rested, they returned to the royal kraal to ask for their orders for the coming day. To their surprise they found that the royal hut was empty, and Ndlovu and Nkalimeva had gone.

"Oh," said the animal children, "while we played, they left for the hills beyond the river, to find the great big moba fields, and Ndlovu took his sleeping mat."

"So *that* was Nkalimeva's game," they cried, and all the fleet of foot gathered in pursuit. In time they caught up with Nkalimeva and their lord.

Nkalimeva fled in fear, but was soon overtaken by the fleet-footed buck. Left and right they charged him with their sharp pointed horns until he slipped away from them at last, and fled to the safety of a large and spreading tree.

"We will send for Nkau to pull him down," his pursuers panted. But the dark was closing in on them, and they settled down to guard him closely packed beneath the tree, so that he would have to tread on them and thus warn them, should he try to escape.

At first he threw small twigs and leaves down on the resting buck to test their watchfulness, but each time they sprang up shouting "He escapes, he escapes!" Finally, he realized that they were too smart for him, so he settled down to sleep.

Now, there are some small gray social spiders (*stegodyphus*) in Africa that live together as many as hundreds at a time in huge gray matted-web homes. It was into a tree occupied by one of these great colonies that Nkalimeva fled.

To pass the time away, his guards whispered and talked among themselves of Nkalimeva's wickedness in trying to entice away their lord.

The small spiders listened and were angry, for, though they were small, they too were Ndlovu's subjects.

Without a sound they crept from their large gray home, and waited for Nkalimeva to sleep—which, in time, he did. Then slowly, softly, and silently they bound him to the tree with their strong gray webs. Round and round they traveled; thicker and thicker grew the bonds that held him, until he looked like a large gray lump on the branch of the tree.

When daylight came, the buck looked up and wondered how he had escaped, for he was nowhere to be seen. Then, far away in the distance, they heard the faint trumpetings of their king, calling them back to duty. Whereupon they stretched their limbs. and obeyed the call of their lord, while the little gray spiders settled down to their feast!

7

FENISANA

KULUMELE's new black baby son was just over two months old, and no longer could she be excused from her daily task of hoeing in the mealie lands. So, putting little Mpabane straddle-legged across her back, she tied him to her with a softly braided goat's skin, knowing that the gentle rhythm of her body as she hoed would rock her little one to slumber.

She had counted without the sun, however, which soon beat down mercilessly from above, and before long Mpabane was screaming his little head off, and was very unhappy indeed.

Whatever should she do? she wondered. The rains were near at hand, and already she had delayed too long in her work.

There was a tree nearby, and the shade beneath its spreading branches was like a huge sunshade held aloft. Kulumele smoothed the little goat's skin in its shade, laid her baby on it, and went back to her hoeing. She sang loudly as she worked, so that her little one would hear her voice, and soon be soothed to slumber.

About a mile away, in a clearing in the thick bush, there lived a troupe of fierce baboons under their cruel leader, Nymphere. Now, one among them was different from the rest: little Fenisana. She was gentle and kind, and loved all the living things around her.

When her companions roughly tortured the small creatures of the wild, Fenisana would snatch them away and nurse them to her breast, setting them free in the safety of the forest.

All the newborn baboon babies were entrusted to her care. She loved their helplessness, and would sit for hours rocking them to and fro in her strange small lap, crooning to them in gruff, kind tones, while the mothers romped and played in their senseless, foolish way.

Therefore it was not so very strange that one day, as she wandered farther afield than usual from the troupe and paused in the shade of the great spreading tree, she seized with joy the sleeping form of Mpabane, while his mother hoed the lands. Gently she rocked him to and fro, making her funny grunting noises to him.

Kulumele, pausing to rest her aching back, glanced upward from her work. With a shriek of fear she dropped her hoe, and rushed toward the tree to snatch her baby from the fearsome creature's grasp.

"Ah," she screamed, "leave my child alone! Who are you?"

To her great surprise the baboon replied, "I am Fenisana. Please let me nurse your child. I love the little thing."

In answer Kulumele snatched Mpabane away, and made all haste back to the kraal.

The following day she found Fenisana waiting for her under the spreading tree, and as he approached, the baboon stretched out her arms and said, "*Please* let me hold your baby while you work. No harm will come to him in my arms. I will guard him for you."

"How strange," thought Kulumele out loud, "She speaks as one of us. Surely she would make a perfect nurse." So she put Mpabane into the baboon's outstretched arms, and all through the morning Fenisana cared for the child.

39

When midday came Kulumele took Fenisana by the hand, and led her to the kraal. There she gave her porridge scrapings and a bowl of curdled milk, and the baboon settled down happily to nurse the child once more.

Soon came the time for the evening meal and Kulumele busied herself with the cooking pot, but when she left the hut to call her lord to eat, she could see no sign of either Fenisana or her baby.

Fearing her husband's anger, she quickly found a long, smooth stone. This she wrapped in a blanket, and slung it baby-wise across her back. Then, pretending that all was well, she called her man to eat.

When all had settled down to sleep (she crooning to the stone from time to time), she quietly arose, and made for the forest, where she knew the fierce Nymphere lived.

All through the dark, unfriendly bush she went, calling at every halt "Fenisana, Fenisana, where have you gone with my child?"

At last from the distance she heard Fenisana reply, "I am here, I am here, and here, too, is your child."

With a cry of joy she stumbled through the darkness in the direction of the voice, and in time she found the clearing in the bush, with the baboons all around, and in the center was Fenisana with her little one.

When she tried to take the child away, however, the big baboons closed in around her, and the chief, Nymphere, caught her roughly by the arm.

"Your little one belongs to us," he cried, "to guide us in your human ways when I am old. The brains of man and strength of us, will make us lords of *all* the beasts.

"I have a feeling, too, for human *flesh*. This I have not tasted since I was young. *Your* meat should be both soft and sweet; tomorrow you will provide us with a sumptuous feast!"

"And if anyone here"—he looked around the circle of his troupe, with wicked, beady eyes—"allows my captive to escape, *theirs* will be the flesh that provides the feast." At these words all his subjects shuddered. He then bade them hold Kulumele, while he bound her tightly with long, strong creepers from the trees.

Throughout his speech little Fenisana wept bitterly. She had not thought that her naughty prank would turn to this. So, when

40

41

SYLVIA BAXTER.

all was quiet, and the others slept, she crept to Kulumele's side, and one by one she gnawed the creepers through with her sharp young teeth. Then, with Mpabane clasped in her arms, she carefully led the way through the sleeping forms, and through the forest to the kraal; and handing the baby to his mother, she silently disappeared.

When Kulumele's husband heard of all that had taken place, he killed his fattest cow in gratitude to Fenisana, and the feasting lasted for many days.

And little Fenisana? She did her best to make amends. Who knows whether or not she escaped the anger of Chief Nymphere? Only the wilds can tell!

8

THE LOVE OF KENELINDA

In a golden valley in the heart of Zululand there lived a man called Thulwane, who had a herd of many cows. Next to his only son, Fana, they were nearest to his heart of all his possessions. Among them there was one more precious than the rest. Her name was Kenelinda.

Her sleek coat shone like gold in the sunshine. Her horns, as long as a man's arm, rose in graceful curves from her pretty head, and two great soft eyes looked out with love upon the world.

No matter how dry the grass, or fierce the winter, she remained fat and glossy, and her milk gushed forth at milking time, so that all around her had their fill. Never had a cow of such size and beauty been known in all the land.

The meat from such a cow, thought all the tribes around, could not fail to be both soft and good. Also to eat the flesh of such a cow would, in turn, make them both strong and good to look upon.

Many had tried to buy Kenelinda by honest means, but Thulwane would not part with her, and daily little Fana took her with the rest of the herd to eat the rich grasses on a nearby hill.

Fana loved Kenelinda with all his little heart. Had she not saved him in his early childhood when the Big Drought struck, and there was no food for man or beast? Always then there had been milk from Kenelinda's never-failing bag, so that the Great Hunger had passed lightly over him. During the years a deep love and understanding had grown between the cow and boy.

Daily, as he took the herd to graze, they walked together, he caressing her from time to time—or when tired, riding on her strong, broad back. He also sang to her and she grew to love his voice, and would acknowledge no other master.

Now one day, when two fierce warriors with cruel eyes and gleaming spears came to Fana on the faraway grazing lands, and demanded his beloved Kenelinda, he knew that resistance would be useless. What could a small defenceless boy do against two such wicked spears?

"Take her," he said after a pause; "you have greater strength than I." And he sat on an anthill to watch them try to take away their prize.

With exclamations of wicked glee, the two men went up to Kenelinda, and hit her on the rump with the flat of their spears, saying, "Hup, hup," to drive her away.

But she would not move.

In anger they turned to Fana and cried, "Your cow is possessed by the Evil One. You who know her make her move, or it will be the worse for you!" Fana replied, "*I* will make her move." Whereupon he went up to her, and with his arms about her neck sang softly in her ear.

> "*Kenelinda, Kenelinda, Kenelinda let us go.*
> *See, they want to kill us, oh, Kenelinda!*"

With a sorrowful look at her little master, she allowed the thieves to drive her away.

"The voice she obeys must go with her," they laughed, prodding

SYLVIA BAXTER.

Fana with their sharp spears as they drove him behind the cow.

About three miles beyond they reached a deep and swiftly flowing river, a raging torrent from bank to bank, and the cow stood still. They could not drive her in.

"Drive your cow across," the wicked thieves threatened, "or our spears will taste your blood." Again Fana's young voice rose, clear and strong this time:

"*Kenelinda, Kenelinda, Kenelinda, go into the water.*
See they want to kill us, oh, Kenelinda!"

As the last word left his lips the cow stepped into the river, and the waters parted. Then they all walked through the river bed to the other side and on into the hills beyond.

In time they reached their captors' home. There they tied Kenelinda to a tree, and together raised their spears to stab her to the heart.

To their bewilderment their freshly sharpened spears refused to pierce the skin, so they turned to Fana in anger, and he sang.

"*Kenelinda, Kenelinda, Kenelinda, soften your skin*
See they want to kill us, oh, Kenelinda!"

The spears went in, and the cow fell down and died.

Sharp knives were then produced and they prepared to skin her for their feast, but the knives refused to cut the skin, and this time Fana had to sing to the dead cow before the knives would go in. So Kenelinda was skinned, and all the meat cut up for roasting.

When all was ready, the thieves and their kin gathered around to eat, but they could not bite the meat because it stuck on their teeth like steel. In great anger now, they turned on Fana to kill him.

Just in time his clear young voice rose once more,

"*Kenelinda, Kenelinda, Kenelinda, soften your flesh*
See, they want to eat you, oh, Kenelinda!"

At this the flesh became as tender as newborn lamb, whereupon they all ate to their hearts' content.

When there was nothing left but the skin and well-picked bones, all settled down to sleep.

When she knew the others slept, an old, old woman drew Fana aside and whispered in his ear, "My child, you are young. I once had one like you, and I would not have you die. These men are cannibals, and when hunger strikes again, *you* will be their meat. Go now with haste while yet they sleep!"

Silently Fana arose, and slipped outside the hut. Carefully he stretched out Kenelinda's lovely skin, with the hair side down. One by one he gathered up her clean-picked bones, and arranged them on the bloody skin, as the full moon shone over the silent night.

When all was done, he folded the skin in place, and lightly tapped it with his herd boy's staff, singing softly as he did so.

> *"Kenelinda, Kenelinda, Kenelinda, wake up,*
> *We will go to our home, oh, Kenelinda!"*

At first the big skin shuddered as he struck it. Then one by one the limbs jerked back to life. As each new move took place, Fana clapped his hands for joy to see his beloved Kenelinda obey his greatest command of all.

Slowly and with care she raised herself, and, with a gentle "moo" as the first breath escaped her lungs, the two slipped through the moonlight into the forest, and were gone.

Next morning, as the sun shed his early brilliance over the awakening countryside, Thulwane, standing in the doorway of his hut, searched the distance with sad and troubled eyes.

At last he gave a shout of joy as he saw, picking their way down the hillside, two figures side by side, and heard Fana's clear young voice, breaking onto the early morning stillness, singing as his father had never heard him sing before.

> *"Kenelinda, Kenelinda, Kenelinda,*
> *See, we are home, oh, Kenelinda!"*

9

NABULELA

For many years Mahlevana, the great chief, had longed for a daughter, but his wives had borne him only sons, so that when his favorite wife at long last presented him with a laughing, black-eyed girl, his joy knew no bounds. There was dancing and feasting in the royal kraal for many days, and all the countryside rejoiced.

She was named Hlalose, the little princess, and throughout her early years Mahlevana gave her all that her heart could wish. He decked her with the gayest beads and she had no equal in all the land.

In time, however, there awoke a burning jealousy in the hearts of all her playmates. Their love turned to envy and hatred as they watched the favors showered on her, though they were careful to hide this from both Hlalose and their chief.

One day, when she had passed her seventh year, the children from the royal kraal went to play at a nearby river, and, as they reached the river's edge, they saw a tiny paw stretched up as if in supplication.

Her little playmates laughed to see a paw foolishly waving in the air, but Hlalose waded quickly into the pool to investigate. There she found a tiny mongrel puppy with a stone tied round its neck, and all but drowned. In haste she took it to the riverbank where she nursed it back to life. Then she carried it gently to her father's hut.

"What is that you carry in your arms, my child?" Mahlevana asked, as his daughter carefully laid the puppy down.

"One of your people wanted to drown this little creature, Baba," she answered, "but I saved it. Now its heart and mine beat as one."

She called her little foundling "Mpempe," and as time passed, closer and closer friends they grew. Never were they apart, and always Mahlevana knew that no harm would befall Hlalose with Mpempe close at hand.

The years passed on, and Hlalose grew into a beautiful happy maiden and Mpempe into an old and feeble dog—too old to follow his beloved mistress daily to fetch the water from the spring.

47

SYLVIA BAXTER.

48

To save his faithful legs while she was on her many daily duties, she left him tied to her father's hut.

It happened one day that all the girls were sent (as is the custom) with earthen pots carried on their heads to the clay pits, to fetch the red ochre to smear on their faces for the tribal dance. Mpempe tried to follow, but the pits were far away, so Hlalose tied him as usual to the hut and, singing the Clay Pot Song, she joined the laughing throng.

On reaching their journey's end, the girls gaily reached down into the deep pit and pulled up lumps of the red clay. Thus they filled their pots.

As they did so, Hlalose's beauty and good humor seemed to fill them with more anger and jealousy than usual. So they whispered among themselves, and made their plan.

As Hlalose reached down to pull up a last handful from the bottom of the pit to cap her brimming pot, they pushed her roughly in, hastily covering her with the earth that lay around the pit, and set off at once for home.

When they came in sight of the kraal, the dog jumped up with ears alert, to greet his beloved mistress, but one by one the girls went by, and no bark of welcome passed Mpempe's lips. Soon he commenced to whine.

The darkness was falling so they all went in to eat the evening meal.

At first none but the dog noticed that Hlalose was not there, but when the chief returned to his hut, he found the thong chewed through, and Mpempe gone.

"This is strange," he said. "Where is Hlalose and why has Mpempe gone?"

No one knew. "No, she did not go with us," the clay gatherers answered. "We heard her speaking of some man she wished to meet at sunset at the water hole," and they made haste away to bed.

Then, as the chief called the men from their huts to light torches and commence a search, Mpempe staggered into sight. His legs were red with clay from toe to shoulder, his head a mask of clay, and in his toothless mouth he grasped a thong from which there hung a little wooden amulet that Hlalose always wore.

"Ah," said the chief, "the girls have lied to me. Carry the faithful Mpempe; he will show the way. His paws have dug deep in clay. Let us hasten to the clay pit," and off they set in haste, blazing torches carried high.

As the clay pit came in sight, the dog commenced to whine, and from a high tree nearby there came a shout of joy, as from its topmost branches Hlalose welcomed them.

There the chief saw proof of what had passed—the hole in which Hlalose had been buried, with claw marks all around where Mpempe had dug his mistress out; and the smears and smudges all over her face where he had licked her back to life.

"Baba," his daughter cried, "then we heard the lions roar, and I made haste to the tree." There, sure enough, were large paw marks of the big cats' paws as they had prowled around the tree.

"But when they saw the flames from the torches as you came, the lions silently slipped away. It was as I climbed the tree that my amulet caught on a branch and fell to the ground. Mpempe seized it and raced to bring you here. Baba, he has more than paid his debt."

Now, when they had returned home once more, Mahlevana called the clay gatherers to him and said,

"Those who give death, receive death, but because Mpempe brought Hlalose back to life, I will give you one chance to redeem your deed. For a long time now it has been my wish to wear the

snow-white skin of the great fierce water beast, Nabulela. Bring him to me, and I will spare your lives."

Nabulela was a huge long-toothed creature that was feared by all. He lived in a small lake not far from the village. To keep him in a good temper, the villagers made flat porridge cakes, and placed them at the water's edge at sunset for the great beast to eat. As they did so, they sang:

> "*Nabulela, Nabulela come out and eat me.*
> *Mahlevana the chief has said,*
> '*Come out and eat me.*' "

There was always a rush and a scramble to get away because Nabulela's favorite food was human flesh, and no man willingly lingered, for fear of being caught. But now the girls had been given a fearsome task. To take Nabulela alive, or kill him? Which should they try to do?

Their hearts sank within them at the thought. However, they made their plans, and all set forth in the afternoon, with a big pot of the usual porridge cakes.

They took care, however, to leave the strong, circular cattle kraal open, both back and front, and they also left four of their number to guard the gates, two at either entrance. Then off the others went, to Nabulela's home.

As the lake came in sight they commenced their song,

> "*Nabulela, Nabulela come out and eat me.*
> *Mahlevana the chief has said,*
> '*Come out and eat me.*' "

Soon from out of the water came an enormous mouth ready to receive the offering. But as the mouth opened wide, the girls saw two toothless jaws, and knew that this was not the creature they sought. So they picked up their porridge cakes, and continued round the lake, at intervals singing their song calling Nabulela to his feast. Many were the creatures who came in answer to their song, but all, as they hopefully opened their large mouths, showed bare and toothless gums.

At last, as darkness descended, there arose from the water a snow-white creature, and in his open mouth huge teeth gleamed.

51

The girls stood their ground, singing their song, and gently drawing farther and farther from the water's edge, pulled the cakes with them while Nabulela followed.

When the fearsome beast was out of the water, they dropped the cakes and ran for home, with Nabulela in close pursuit. They ran with speed, but the great beast's legs were strong, and slowly and surely he gained on them.

Just as their breath had all but failed them, the village came in sight. Straight through the strong round cattle kraal they ran, and as they passed through the farthest gate, their friends pushed in the heavy posts as Nabulela sniffed their heels. He turned to reach the gate through which he had already passed, but *that* had been closed behind him, and he found himself a captive in the big round kraal.

Then came the fathers of the girls with shields and gleaming spears to finish their daughters' work and thus save them from the chief's anger. In time their numbers wore the great beast down, and Nabulela sank bleeding to the ground.

So it was that until his death Mahlevana wore Nabulela's snow-white skin as a cape across his shoulders, and the clay gatherers were forgiven.

Still, in the faraway villages in Zululand, the little ones ask for the song of Nabulela to soothe them to their slumber.

10

THE SONG OF THE DOVES

Somakhehla's heart was full of sorrow, for Nombakatholi, his much loved wife, was barren, and it seemed that he would go childless to his grave. Who could have a light heart with such a thought to dog his footsteps?

Nombakatholi loved Somakhehla with all her heart, and her failure to bear him children brought great unhappiness to her. Nightly she cried herself to sleep in the solitude of her hut.

The crops, however, had to be planted, for the rains had commenced, and Phezukomkhono (Piet-my-vrou, the red-breasted cuckoo) called incessantly for her to till the fields. So she took her hoe, and set about her task with a heavy heart.

The sun was shining brightly after the rain and *all* the birds, not only Phezukomkhono, were singing. There was so much happiness around her, that she beat her head with her hands and cried out to two doves flying overhead, that had been making the morning sweet with their gentle cooing,

"Oh, why should I alone be sad today?"

To her great surprise the doves answered her saying,

"And why *ARE* you sad?"

"It is because I am barren, and there is no child to bring laughter to my lord and me," she replied.

"Mfune! Mfune! Mfune!" they chanted as they dropped from above, taking their places, one on either side of her. "Pick us up," they cooed, arching their pretty necks, "and take us to your home. There we will tell you of the magic that will bring fulfilment to your wish."

Gently Nombakatholi lifted the little doves from beside her, and tucking one under each arm, made haste back to her hut.

Once inside, she carefully fastened the door, so that none should see or hear what took place inside; and when she had seated herself on the floor, the little doves once more took their positions, one on either side of her.

"Make a bed within the earthen pot that stands against the wall," they cooed.

As in obedience she did their bidding, there was a chorus of "*Mfune! Mfune!*" from the trees around the hut. Surely all the doves in the world had gathered there to add their songs of praise to the Great One above!

"Cover it with care, and do not look within until the moon has gone to rest," chanted the doves, and their friends once more took up the song.

When she had followed their instructions, she took them from the dimness of the hut into the beautiful sunshine of the spring morning, and as they rose into the air they called back to her, "Watch your pot, and tell no one of what has passed today until the time is ripe. Mfune! Mfune!" And they were lost to sight.

As the grey dawn broke on the following day, she lifted the lid of her big grain pot, and looked inside. A sob of joy came from her lips as she saw, lying on the little goatskin bed, the dimpled body of a baby girl.

The little one stretched up her arms, and for the first time in many moons, Nombakatholi's joyous laughter filled the hut.

She called the baby Fihliwe (The Hidden One) and as the years passed, she grew apace both in beauty and in kindliness, and her mother kept her secret safe from all. When Nombakatholi worked by day, she had little Fihliwe in the big grain pot, leaving sorrow marks around her hut, so that none would enter there.

Somakhehla puzzled from time to time at voices coming from the hut at night when mother and daughter played, and sometimes at the sound as though a baby cried. He asked Nombakatholi what caused these sounds.

"Ah! my lord," she sighed, "I often converse with myself at the sorrow that is mine, that I should be barren. Sometimes, too, I cry at my childless state." Knowing the ways of women he was satisfied.

As Fihliwe grew in beauty and in years, so she grew in grace, until, when she had reached the marriage age, she was more lovely than all the maidens in the land, and Nombakatholi felt that the time had come to make her secret known.

She therefore dressed Fihliwe in the gayest beads, whilst in her hair she twined flowers from the forest, and sent her to the water-hole, to draw water with which to cook the mid-day meal.

Now, the great Mveli, much loved chief of all the land, was standing by the water-hole to watch his royal cattle slake their thirsts, as Fihliwe with downcast eyes and water pot upon her head passed him by.

She raised her eyes and, as his gaze met hers, the great chief's heart stood still. Such beauty he had never seen, and he was tongue-tied as he looked upon her sweetness.

At last he found his voice and said, "My pretty one, your face is strange to me. Do you come from far afield and who do you visit here?"

"I am Somakhehla's daughter," she said, shyly casting down her lovely eyes.

"But that *could* not be," Mveli said, "Somakhehla is a childless man. Come, child, tell me your name."

"I know no other hut than that of Nombakatholi, Somakhehla's wife," she insisted, and a gentle cooing filled the air as her guardian doves circled round her head, as she passed along the pathway to her home.

Mveli stood as though he had been turned to stone; then, when he had found his voice once more, called his headman to him.

"Follow that maiden to her father's huts," he commanded. "I would have her as my foremost wife."

Therefore, when the headman saw Fihliwe enter Nombakatholi's hut, he took the tidings to Mveli.

"Prepare a fitting gift, and take it to the father of the girl," said the chief, "and let him know my wish."

Carrying Mveli's gift in his hand, the headman went to the Village Council tree, and there he gave Mveli's message to Somakhehla.

"I am a man of sorrow!" said the old man, beating his hands upon his chest; "I have no child to bring blessings to me in my old age, nor to fulfil the wishes of your lord."

It was then that Nombakatholi called her husband to her and told him the strange story of the kindness of the doves, and how the birds' magic had given them their child. Then she brought Fihliwe out for him to see. He too, was left speechless, and held his hands before his eyes as though her beauty blinded him.

In joy he turned to those near to him and said, "Tonight we feast. Kill my fattest cow, and let preparations be made." Then, returning to Mveli's headman he said, "I gladly give Fihliwe to your lord."

Now, as Nombakatholi heard her husband's words, she brought out her roll of woven mats. These she unrolled from the doorway of her hut right down the pathway that led to the Council tree where Mveli's headman sat, and bade Fihliwe walk with pride along their path for all to see—a fitting bride for Mveli's royal kraal.

11

THE MARRIAGE FEAST

It happened long ago, in a faraway Zulu village, that while a dance was at its gayest, a tall young man of great beauty was seen dancing among the rest. Now as little Nkongwe's eyes fell upon him, she felt that no other suitor would satisfy her. She therefore went to her parents, and asked them to make inquiries as to his presence there.

"I come," he said, "to seek a bride among your many lovely maidens. My home is far away, beyond the hills, but a good bride price awaits the father of the one I choose."

They invited him to their guest hut, and treated him as a favored one. The more Nkongwe saw of him, the more in love with him she fell, and the more she assured her parents that no other suitor would satisfy her. So that in time arrangements were made for their marriage.

With a great deal of celebrating and merrymaking the wedding took place, and Nkongwe and her husband settled down happily in the village, tilling their lands and planting their crops, until the husband said that the time had come to celebrate the marriage in his own home. Nkongwe was delighted, and gladly agreed to go with him.

It happened that Nkongwe had a little brother named Khok-hoba, who could not take his eyes off the tall, good-looking stranger, and, on the day of their departure, as his sister made ready for the journey, her bridegroom said, "The day is hot, I will wash myself at the river, ready for the journey."

Now Khokhoba was an inquisitive boy. "Here," he thought, "is my chance to see *more* of this beautiful man. I will follow him to the river. Perhaps I, too, could bring such gloss and beauty to my skin could I but learn his secret before he goes."

This he did, silently and stealthily, hiding behind a bush close to the water's edge, and watched as he made ready for his bath. To his horror and dismay he saw the stranger carefully slip out of his soft chocolate-colored skin, to show beneath the rough hairy body of a big black baboon!

With a gasp of fear he turned and ran for home with all the speed he could raise, and straightway went to his sister's hut, where he told her of his dreadful findings.

However, no matter how often he assured her of what he had seen, she would not believe that her husband was a wicked baboon in disguise. Therefore, when he had returned from his bath and all was ready, she set off with him with joy for her new home over the hills.

57

Khokhoba was very fond of his sister, and not wishing any harm to befall her, followed close behind, and in time he showed himself, begging to be allowed to accompany them. Since neither Nkongwe nor her husband had any objections, they did not turn him back, and the three went on together.

It was a long walk, and as they penetrated deeper and deeper into the wild and lonely country, Khokhoba became more and more afraid, pulling on his sister's arm from time to time, trying to turn her back. But she dragged her arm impatiently away, and on they went, reaching in time a collection of rough and ragged huts none of which had doors. They were all empty.

"Now," said the stranger, "you must wait for me in this hut, while I go to gather in my people for the marriage feast." When they were safely inside, he pushed large rocks into the doorway so that they could not get out.

In haste Khokhoba pulled aside some of the grass with which the hut was thatched in time to see the bridegroom quickly slip from his outer skin and in his baboon form set off toward the nearby forest.

He called his sister to his side, and she was just in time to see the hairy form disappear into the trees.

He was a strong little boy, and with great speed he cut a hole in the roof with a knife that he had snatched from his father's hut before he left.

Pulling Nkongwe after him, he set off with haste along a track in the opposite direction to that which the baboon had taken to call his friends. They soon came to a deep and swiftly flowing river, fringed with reeds, that barred their way. Again the boy's sharp knife went to work, and with speed he made a buoyant raft from the long hollow reeds, tied together with strong creepers.

Onto this they threw themselves as a large troupe of angry baboons, with cries of rage, burst through the tangle on the bank.

"Come back, come back to the marriage feast!" the wicked leader cried.

"Our raft is heavy, and we cannot make it move," cried Khokhoba. "Plait a rope of creepers, and throw it to us, that you may pull us to you." Meanwhile he tried to work the raft into the midstream current.

58

- SYLVIA BAXTER.

59

Slowly it responded to his efforts, and by the time the baboons had made the creeper rope, the first fast waters had caught the flimsy craft.

With a mighty heave the big baboon threw the rope, while his friends held on behind, and together brother and sister caught and tied it to the raft.

Swiftly now the water bore them on. But as you know, when a simian's hand closes on a thing, he *cannot* let it go; and so one by one the currents sucked them in, and one by one it pulled them under and drowned them all, while Nkongwe and her brother floated on.

In time they reached a bank they knew, and there they caught the trees in passing, pulling themselves ashore, and thus were saved.

12

THE RIVER MAIDEN

IT is a long time ago now since this happened but we all know that Monya, the python, is the guardian of the river, and that, even though he sometimes hunts in the forests, he always returns to his home in the deep and silent pool to watch over Nonkhosi, his beloved foundling.

Have you not seen the whirlwind clutch and scatter all in its path? And the howling gale send all to seek the cover of their huts? Then you all know that River Guardian visits River Guardian, and this is his sign that he walks abroad.

It is a strange parent who does not love its young, but once it happened that there was such a man. He had two daughters. Nomkhosi, the first-born, found no place in her father's heart, and for a long time he made plans to do away with her.

Somate was his "little one," and he gave to her the love of two. Somate, however, loved her elder sister, and was never happier than when they played together. This raised great jealousy in her father's heart, so one day he took Nomkhosi by the hand, saying, "Daughter, come and walk with me."

Down to the river he led her, and as they reached the water's edge, he bound her hands behind her, and threw her into a deep and silent pool.

Down and down she sank, and as she reached the bottom, the python saw her struggling form.

"Ah!" he said, "here is food for many days." He smacked his lips and approached the drowning child, to twine his great coils around her body, and squeeze her shape to fit his cruel jaws. But as he gazed on her sweet young face, he changed his mind.

"Why should I not give her the immortality of the river?" he thought, "and keep her here forever? She shall be our River Maid." And he swam close to her, wrapping his great coils around her to keep her body still. Thus he held her gently while he gazed into her face and mesmerized her, as a python does his prey to bend their will to his.

Thus Nomkhosi became one of the river folk. Throughout the day she played with her new friends, the fishes, the crabs, and many others. Even the wicked crocodile grew to love her, while the great river swelled with pride to think that of all the rivers in the land, none other had for its own a human maid.

When the darkness came at night, she was tenderly cradled in the loving coils of Monya's long and scaly body.

However, little Somate pined for her big sister, and daily asked her father where she was. But he answered her roughly, telling her to "go ask the fishes."

So, when the women went to draw water at the river one day, she went with them, and as she wandered from the others, she peered into the deep, silent pool to ask the fishes this question, and she saw her sister's laughing face.

"Sister," she cried, "what are you doing there? There is no happiness for me in our home without you. Come back to us! And how is it that you can live beneath the water? Let me come and join you!"

But Nomkhosi begged Somate to go home without her, saying, "I am happy here, where all the creatures love me. Go home, little sister, and tell no one of what you have seen today."

All day long Somate nursed her secret, but when night came her loneliness became too much for her, and she said to her father, "Baba, I have seen my sister, playing with the fishes at the bottom

61

of the big and silent pool. There is no happiness in life for me without her. Let us bring her home, or I will join her there."

Now, the father had no wish to lose his favorite child, so when the morning came, together they went to the water's edge, and bade Nomkhosi to return with them. They took her home, and once more little Somate laughed and sang, and was happy all day long.

But the river was very angry when he found that he had lost his River Maid, and, as the wind whipped up the wavelets, they splashed with angry mutterings against the bank.

"We will fetch our foundling back," roared the river, and with a great upward surge the water swirled over the bank, with Monya riding on its crest, as together they advanced towards the father's hut.

They forced open the door with their mighty strength, and so gained entrance to the hut. Gently Monya gathered up the sleeping maid in his great coils, and, still riding on the wave, returned to the deep and silent pool once more.

And there Nomkhosi lives until today, the river's beloved maiden.

SYLVIA BAXTER.

GLOSSARY

Witch doctor: A man looked upon as having supernatural powers. There are good ones and bad ones.

Ntunjambili: Ntoo-nja-mbee-lee.

"Smell out": A term meaning *find out*, used in connection with a witch doctor's supposedly supernatural powers.

"It was many moons": A moon means a period of time, i.e. a month.

Xhosa: A tribe adjoining the Zulus.

Hyena: A large spotted type of wild dog, very much despised for its sneaking, cowardly habits. Parts of it are used by witch doctors in their supernatural dealings.

Selesele: Se-le-se-le (e as in English).

Ncinci: Ncee-ncee.

Maluzwane: Mah-loo-zwa-ne.

Segege: See-ge-ge.

Mhlope: White. M-slaw-pe.

Fudu: Foo-doo.

Mabele: Type of small round grain. Mah-be-le.

Makhanda: Heads. Mah-kah-ndah.

The bones were thrown: Like the term "throw the dice." A witch doctor will throw a collection of especially selected bones in a certain manner, and the pattern in which they fall will indicate to him the guilty one or the chosen one.

Bridal beadwork: In those days the women wore little besides a string skirt and many bead ornaments.

Nkau: Monkey. Nkah-woo.

"Our pits are full": Zulu people used to store their grain in underground pits.

Kraal: Village.

Mpabane: Mpah-bah-ne.

Nymphere: A name. Nee-mfe-re.
   The Zulu mothers carry their babies slung on their backs, held by a goat's (braided) skin, or cloth, tied in front. Babies are carried in this manner almost from birth.

Thulwane: Too-lwah-ne.

Hlalose: Slah-law-se. Meaning "she who sits always."

Baba: Father. Bah-bah.

Somakhehla: Som-ke-slah.

Mpempe: Whistle. Mpe-mpe.

Nombakathole: Nom-bah-kah-taw-le.

"Mfune, Mfune!": Cooing of doves. Mfoo-ne.

Fihliwe: Fee-slee-we. Meaning the Hidden One.

Sorrow marks: Signs proclaiming that there is sorrow within the hut, therefore not to enter.

A good bride price: Among the Bantu people, wives are an expensive matter, the would-be husband paying many cattle, or up to £100 ($300) or more, to the father of the bride. All this is not necessarily paid before the marriage, and is returned by the father if the marriage is not satisfactory.

Khokhoba: Kaw-kaw-bah.

Nomkhosi: Nom-koh-see.

Somate: Soh-mah-te.

The Zulu "i" is pronounced ee	as in English "see".
The Zulu open "e" is pronounced e	as in English "ere".
The Zulu closed "e" is pronounced ay	as in English "hay".
The Zulu "a" is pronounced ah	as in English "ah!"
The Zulu open "o" is pronounced aw	as in English "paw".
The Zulu closed "o" is pronounced oh	as in English "low".
The Zulu closed "u" is pronounced oo	as in English "soon".